Feeling This Way

Ben Esqueda

Dear world,

To whomever is reading this wherever you are standing in this world: we all have something in common. We all have a heart that beats approximately 100,000 times a day. We all have loved and lost in our own unique ways. We all have felt butterflies as well with our hearts dropping and stopping simultaneously. Even if we love in different ways, it is that very same heart in our bodies we all have.

Aside from that, we look up at the same sky. Whether it is grey and rainy on your end and sunny and blue on mine, it is the same. With that being said, with the same heart comes the same feelings, just different stories of how we felt those feelings.

For me, the reflection I would see in the mirror my entire life was my biggest enemy. I have been in a constant battle with my own heart and for who it feels for. I hated myself designed in my true colors, so I painted my life in black and white for the longest time. We live in a generation so accepting, yet it took twenty-one years for my very own heart to accept itself. I have learned to love that I am not normal, and if I am being honest, it felt like I went to space the first time I kissed a boy. Years into genuinely accepting every root of my heart, I then met a soul that made me feel something I have never experienced: instant vulnerability. It was the most alluring and helpless feeling I have ever felt. For the first time I fought harder than I ever have and tried my absolute hardest to make something work that never added up equivalently. To make the story short, I had to say goodbye, and that is when a bittersweet pain was born.

I hated myself for limiting the miles I would go for someone I loved. But in the last miles, I ended up eating my heart alive to hold onto the love between us. To put it simply, that is not what love should be. But very soon after I realized that even though I had lost him, I still had rooms in my soul I still had to fill with my own flowers. This book holds every root and chapter in my story. The way I could not stand the truth of who I wanted to love then, all the way up to it being my favorite part of my heart. From loving someone the hardest I could into hurting the worst I ever have. I not only wrote these words to heal myself but to heal and help you as well. Though we may feel lonely during difficult times, it is also comforting to know we all feel the same feelings.

From inside the secrets of my heart.................................. 2

I love me, please love you... 14

A heart struck by a lightning bolt.................................... 38

Drifting souls... 60

Locking it in the vault 98

Coming of age tranquility... 138

From inside
the secrets of
my heart

Wanting people to love me for me and wanting my own heart to believe that I am enough. Hiding my favorite colors in me because it is not "normal." Constantly dipping myself in black paint to mask it all. But sometimes, people come into my life and find a way to wipe the black away to find the sincere colors. Life never feels finer than when that happens.

16 & alone

I have been accidentally looking at my own gender in a romantic way. I despise the way my heart feels for a friend of mine, and most importantly, I despise that my heart feels this way for a boy. I cannot fathom that my true heart is wrong for our society. I have convinced the world I am normal, but under the surface of my skin I know I am different. I tell myself it is much easier to live this life in a lie, but is it really a life if I am dying inside?

I am in a generation of acceptance, yet I do not accept myself.
I listen to everyone's heart with open ears, but I ignore my own.
I preach to everyone to not fear, but I look in the mirror and feel insecure.
I tell those around me to be no one but themselves, but I want to be anyone but myself.
I tell her I love her, but I am whispering the same words to him.

I want to feel the sun
The way you do
The way you smile with grace
Even when madness interrupts you

It is a scary time.

Life is changing faster than ever, and my own mind feels unrecognizable. My mother once told me to always listen to my heart, but I can no longer hear it. We preach about how we need to love ourselves, but we act the opposite when the lights are off. The grass is not greener on the other side, and the sun no longer kisses my skin the way it used to.

All so the world will not look at me any less
All so the world will be impressed
All so the world will not see my mess

I will feed you my lies
I will never confess

We live in a society where
Happiness is defined by our shell
And body weight
Only to make us body-hate

We get satisfaction
When we improve
In places where we think we lack

We are afraid to love today
Because we fear tomorrow
We live in a society where
Insecurities shine brighter than confidence

Overflowing with such dramatic feelings
But I present myself dull

I fought against my truth
And attempted to live in my lies
My entire life

This is not just another hand
This is another man's hand in mine
And for the first time ever
I felt the way they feel in romcoms
And for the first time ever
I want to take you home to my family and show you off

I know they will find you lovely
You do not try, you just do
You do not overthink, you are just you

I love me, please love you

Please understand me.

I am done lying to not only you
But to myself too
I am done looking away
From what truly pleases my eyes

I want to vocalize my love
I am done writing love stories
And keeping it a secret
I finally want the world to see it

I will no longer lock the doors of my heart
And call him… her
This has not been easy
Please understand me

When I first held your hand in public
It felt like
The feeling I pushed away
For a lifetime
Charged at me and defeated me
In the best way

Walls crumbling down
Doorways kicked down
Your lightning struck
My darkest fears

I used to be.

I used to be scared of the water of love
I would always admire the view
But never go for a swim

But then came someone special
Teenage hearts and a bright moon
Impulsive love and careless actions

With you by my side
Judgment fell beneath my feet
And just like that
My heart was finally in the water of love
For the very first time

My father said
Show people who you really are
My mother said
I am never going to stop loving you

Moments after that
I shed my old skin
The way I walked became more authentic
The way I saw the world became graceful

You are sitting in your car
The lights are bright on the highway
You look out the window
Seeing cars, houses, and mountains
Seeing everything pass by you
A blur of vision
And it seems as if it is too fast

That is a representation of life
It is all a little too fast
And it might slip away
So take a grip on it all
Before it is too late

We have all been destroyed
We have all stood up strong in rain
We have all seen the clouds shift away
And seen the sun shift in

Ultimately it is up to us
How we share ourselves
The way we give and receive compliments
The conversations that we make
And all the things we believe in

There could be ten things
Going wrong in a room
But you could be the one right thing
That calms and replenishes it all

A story about strength

You have a story behind your eyes
The scars inside your heart define your history
The skip in your step
And the way you hold your chin up
Spells strength
Your smile is a sun of its own
It magnifies the light you carry internally

It is important to have weak moments. Certain joy rides will end, and it is okay to take a dip in your river of ancient tears. It is important to acknowledge the worst of you as well as the best of you. It is okay to build a foundation, and down the road you want to break it down and start over. Sleepless nights that end in repetitive night drives because the wheel feels like it is the only thing you have control of in life.

All of the roots inside of you are alluring.

A mirror can be your worst enemy
The way your body image affects you
The way you can convince yourself
That you are not enough

But see, the thing is
A mirror can become a window
Of new limits and new perspectives
Speak motivation into yourself
Instead of breaking yourself down

No more of letting it reflect back at you
Break the barriers and see past it all

Life feels off beat
And your tunes do not soothe you like before
You are stuck in the corner
You feel like you cannot move

It has come to the point where
Your tears are no longer falling
But your heart is sinking

This is your most raw self
This is the start to healing
You will be better

Loving only what the world wants me to

Your legs on the dashboard
I never had a feeling like this before
I often think
How pretty life would not be
If I never came across you

Do you ever meet a soul
And you think to yourself and say
"This is what I needed
This is what life is about
This is what joy feels like
Even on the bad days"

Words were designed
To be powerful and leave an impact
Have a voice defined by integrity
Have conversations and be attentive
Last but not least:
Love with the right intentions

An old soul with a young heart
Mature but not experienced
Trying to accept something in myself
That the world finds different

You might not know the reason
Behind the answer
You might not have the words
To explain the way you feel

Through the process
You might have some nights
Where you feel like
Who you love is a curse
Rather than a blessing
And when you cannot sleep
Pray and take deep breaths

Fearful to fearless.

I have always wondered what it felt like to confidently hold the hand of my same gender in the middle of a crowd. To love a man so strongly that wandering eyes and judgmental words did not faze anything.

I was the boy in the crowd that held judgment and envied the same-gender couples. But only because underneath myself was boiling lava that could not erupt because of fear—of the things people would say, and the different ways my family might love me.

But then the unthinkable happened: I am now the man in the crowd. I am an erupting volcano of celebration, holding a man's hand. Fear is erased, and the crowd around us is chanting for us.

I always dreamt of my significant other
On our wedding day
High heels and a dreamy dress
Someone I had the honor to call my wife
For the rest of my life

But then I grew
And my dream got reborn
For me,
A forever after
Meant man and man

My past dreams were built with
What the world wanted for me
Instead of what I needed for me
It is his lips
Not her lips
It is his touch
Not her touch

Free

Twenty-two years old now
At a coffee shop in Texas
I am no longer enemies with my heart
In fact, we are best friends now

It speaks out loud, fearlessly
And not just written on paper anymore
I told my family
And the humans that mean the most to me

Around me there is
A live band to my left
A lake in front of me
The moon replaced the sun
I finally feel peace and serenity
I finally feel like life has begun

Growth is power.

Time will teach.

Nothing is heavier than
Living inside a heart that only you know

There is nothing fulfilling about
Watching the world
Love a version of you
That is built on a false narrative

For once, give in to your heart
Instead of the ones around you

Be honest with yourself
Be loyal to the words
That speak inside your mind
Admire your authentic self

Incomplete is acceptable
Bad days are acceptable
Broken is acceptable

But when you feel these ways
Remember to focus on self-care
And the closer you will get to completeness
The good days will follow
Shortly after the bad ones
And broken just means more alluring

A love letter to myself

Everything beneath the surface is even more beautiful. Scars do not mean damage; they mean healing and strength. When life feels burdensome, take it easy on your mind.

Patterns sometimes change, and the good runs away. They might not text you back and traffic will bother you more than usual. Some questions may never be answered, but there is an answer in that. It is important to take a second to feel your very own heartbeat.

You should always be enough.

I think the ultimate answer is to be in love with life. I have come across elderly couples that seem as if their love has grown more each day. Behind their many stories and aged bodies, they make it seem like the numbers vanish.

Walks at the park, home-cooked meals, and their favorite songs that remind them both of when the love first sparked.

In love with life.
In love with each other.

It is a brave movement
To love who you love

To not let fear
Be greater than what is sincere

It is okay
To touch lips in sunlight
And no longer just
Under the sheets at night
It is okay
To squeeze their hand at the dinner table
To be able
To be vocal

As strangers' eyes pan over
To something different
Be proud that you are that

To watch you grow
And accept the roots
You once attempted to pull out

I smile with tears in my eyes
Finally seeing you smile
And living a life with no more lies

To see you embrace
And not feel like a disgrace
To seeing you live
And not just getting by

A heart struck by a lightning bolt

August 28 . 2020 x Palm Springs

To my luv,

They say the greatest things come into your life when you least expect them. It is a phrase I have always heard, but never seemed to fully believe in. That was until I was in Palm Springs on a sunny day with my friends and you walked in the door. You swept me off my feet and your eyes had not spotted me yet. I was introduced to you and my heart instantly felt weaker (in a good way). The entire day my focus was on you and my mind wanted to do nothing but ask and listen to your life story.

The moon has replaced the sun, and we have not only met, we have not left each other's sight.
We are in the pool together, laughing and by each other's side. I could not figure out if you were glancing at me in a romantic way or in a friendly way. We continued to sip on cocktails, and as the conversations continued between you and me, it felt as if our hearts both knew and felt this foreign feeling we both never experienced before.

It's 12am now and we are still in the pool together. Coincidentally both of our glasses were empty at the same time, so we both got out of the pool and made our way to the bar. As you were making our drinks I accidentally looked at you a little too long, and the second you glanced back I turned away. This feeling in me was bringing with it the biggest amount of fear yet the greatest amount of adoration.

Instead of going back to the pool, you led the way into your hotel room. As I sat on your bed my head was spinning about the ideas I had and feelings I felt for you, all in one day of meeting you. Without speaking, it was like we both felt the same exact emotions. The ones I have only imagined and felt in my dreams were the ones I was feeling for you, in real life.

You were shuffling through your clothes and taking off your shoes. Not a single word was exchanged, but I heard both of our hearts screaming for one another. A few minutes have passed; I am on your bed and you finally made your way to me. It is like you were walking to me in slow motion and suddenly our lips were together. A storm of butterflies filled the room, and we were under the blankets. I could not count the times my heart stopped and fluttered as I kissed you and held you for the very first time. I was afraid that if I fell asleep, I would wake up and you would just be a dream. Lastly I thought to myself, "Oh, this is what love is."

Show me what you are made of
Tell me how many times you have been in love
Tell me about the boys and girls
That hurt you
And how you grew

Let's laugh about your favorite family memories
And all the secrets you kept in your diaries
Let me hold you close
Not only in the easy times
But during the hard times too

Let's be lonely together
Let's turn our hardships
Into something alluring

Dinner table tension -

The lights are dim
My seat next to yours
My chest is tight
My hands are shaking
You think your mother across from us
Is oblivious to what this is
But I can see in her eyes
She senses the truth behind your lies

I am a special friend of yours at the table
But my hand is intertwined with yours underneath
The dinner table is quiet
And eventually, our plates start to clear
Then your mother begins to spill the love story
Between your father and her

As she chokes up on certain details of her story
About how her heart fell
I fight my tears from falling as well

In this moment, I begin to realize
The vulnerability in her words
Is the same way you speak yours

When the sun sets low
And the stars shine bright
I really hope you know
It is us against the world
And when you feel like life is falling apart
It is falling together

While I am learning from you
I also want to love you
As each new day approaches

I want us to be
More authentic and raw
Each day our heads lift off our pillows

Three ways you changed me.

You made my laugh a little louder
You were all of my favorite love stories in one
You made my smile a little brighter

Out of all the bad, I chose the good and this is why:

You love my heart including the flaws / You look at me in a way I never thought someone would / You are the first human that crosses my mind when a love song comes on / You gave me the same comfort as my baby blanket / Each time I run into your arms chaos turns into to comfort

You are asleep next to me
We are both from the same home town
But I think we made a home out of each other

I cannot fathom
That you took all of my hidden ghosts
And made them dance

When I close my eyes and hold you
I pray that we fly high
Instead of fall low
I pray that we make it out okay
Instead of walking one by one
Alone

You do a magnificent job at pretending
We were never anything
But I know the second you are alone
In your thoughts
Your stomach is in a million knots
And you feel at loss

If only you spoke your thoughts
And I spoke mine

As we ran into the ocean at 1am, there were chills over my entire body, but my hand was warmer than ever wrapped in yours. Our toes could not touch the sand beneath the waves, our bodies were drifting but our hearts were connecting. Salty kisses that somehow tasted sweet.

A new month means a new chapter
The same love but just a bit stronger
Disagreements drawn in
Only to become closer
Young and in the middle of the wild
You are my special four-leaf clover

My favorite boy in sight
Kisses at red lights
The roads we chose
And the turns we took
I would not want it any other way

A comfortable love
Where you wear what you wear
Because you are who you are
The fake laughs vanish
And the shallow questions
Drift into deep confessions

We have never been able to finish a movie
Because our lips
Always find a way to touch
I know your deepest secrets
You know my biggest insecurities

I adore the way
A storm of conversations erupts
The second our heads hit the pillows
You take me into another world
With your stories
You make me feel like a kid again
With no worries

All in three months

You opened up more than you ever have
In your entire life, to me
You shared the experiences that broke you
And the monsters that scare you
The stories we told and the love we shared
It all grew so fast-maybe even too fast

I remember all of your favorite things
The way you like your back scratched
The moments when light exploded into your eyes
Your favorite dinner spots
And so much more
Just like my favorite movie lines
They are all engraved in my mind

All in three months
I unlocked the gates to your true heart
You saw me as your everything
And I could never picture life apart
Your tears have become just as contagious
As your laugh
And that is when I knew

I know my heart felt those three words
As soon as you walked through those doors

Even though today is not the day
You will hear the words I am dying to say
Just know
I will fight through whatever comes our way

When you are weak
I will come in strong
When you are doubtful
I will come in prideful
As new days appear
And life changes
Our love will remain the same
And grow even greater

The way you hear me
The way you heal me

You make me feel like I am something

You give my heart a childhood playground
It is the way you make my heart skip a beat
And how afraid I am to blink
I do not want to miss a single thing

You decorated the home of my soul
So beautiful
So remarkable

You make Christmas feel year-round
I catch myself smiling at absolutely nothing

I wake up each day in disbelief
At how something so rare
Is sharing a life with me

With you I learned
That paradise is not a place
It is a feeling

The world is crashing and burning
Every aspect
Every city
Flames in front of me

Then I see you in the middle of the fire
Waiting for my hand
To go through it all in faith that
We will not burn
We will put out the flames
Together

Out of all the things we say
All the things we do
All the ways we love

My favorite thing is
A room alone, with you
Lights dim
Candles lit
Bottles empty
Glasses full
Shirts undone

My dearest love

Drifting souls

Like a storm
The power
Like the rain
It dried
Like the clouds
It drifted

I was dancing in the sky
You were sitting back
Watching it all die
You were living ahead of time
Knowing the wreckage

I feel that you are not well
But you say that you are fine
I feel as if we are at the end of the line

My soul never had the capacity
For the miles I would have traveled
For you
And I hope you knew
All the storms I would have
Held your hand through

Reading you was like
Reading a book backwards
The double life rotted away the passion in us
I was so sure I could scrape away your rust
Please find a flame to light your candle
So you can make a home out of me

To me, love is love
But as our hands touched
In the middle of the street
The people stopped and stared

I held on tighter
You released
I did not care
You did
I learned
You ignored
I stayed
You ran

I was listening to sad tunes in my car
I made it to my home town
Knowing you were here too
It was a hard time, it was a hard night
I bought a beer from a store near
I parked my car and
I glanced up at the night sky
And saw the biggest shooting star of my life

I spent the entire night wondering if it was a sign
To reach out and realign
Or to validate my heart
That we are better off apart

Do you hear my heart
During your times of silence
Or have we changed
And become unrecognizable?

Calling every name in my phone
I am afraid of being alone
Searching for a voice like yours
But none of them come close
All of my friends say to forget about you
And that my heart deserves more
But if more is not you
I do not want it

Do you have weak moments like this too?
Or have you already met someone new?

One last night alone, together

This love grew old quick
There is not much left of us

For one last night
Hold me tight
For one last night
Kiss me right
For one last night
Stay in my sight

When the sun peeks out
The sky will glow
We will know
That it is time to let go

Your hands around me at night
Do not feel the same
Your kisses are tasteless
Our conversations are dull

The last conversation we had
You thought I was closing up
But I was choking up
My words were weak because I was scared
Of the developing truth in front of my eyes

When the secret of us got out
To a dear friend of yours
I knew your insecurities had kicked in
And your heart felt exposed
We were in different cities
But with the way you were speaking
I could tell your heart closed

I hate the idea
Of you tiptoeing away from what made you the happiest
Just to make the people around you happy

The what ifs and what they will say
Ate it all away
You used to beg to hold me at night
Now I do not think you will care if I stay
You do not grab my hand in car rides anymore
Why do you not feel warm
Like you did before?

I have learned
To not take words to heart
And that is where the hurt start
My love was written in pen
Yours was in pencil

It all might be erased
But in certain sunlight
I can see the indents of your old words
I can feel the memories
Of what it was

You said we were missing something
But deep down inside
You know you feel nothing

It is the words we say
That are out of line
It is the way we pretend
Like everything is fine
You were the one that came on too strong
Now you are saying this is wrong

The world is still spinning
As well as my mind
Even if I had the worst part of us
I would still graciously run with it

How did we get here
How do we get back
To the times where
We would laugh
To the times where
Our love was innocent?

When did I become the person
That you hid stories from?
Who you no longer shared the details of your days to
When did I become a chore
Instead of a pleasure
When did your heart become a maze?
Please tell me the way
Please stay

I abused my own heart
By choosing the fantasy
And ignoring the reality

Wounds all over my skin
I hold up a drained face
My pain has turned numb
But maybe feeling nothing
Is better than feeling everything

I once was a trophy
Now just change on the floor
Waiting for someone to want me

I want the little things back

I want to feel the rush in my heart
When I see your car pull in my driveway
I want to hear your morning voice
Telling me to get up for coffee
I want to hear your knock on my door
To melt in your arms

I want you to wake me up
In the middle of the night
Only to make sure I am still in your sight

You were fond of my pretty
But you despised my ugly
You stood up brave
To hide away the love you crave

Our love fell to the ground
And broke into pieces
I suffocate
So you can breathe
I hold back
So you can be free

You say that you want to breathe again
When I was once the air to your lungs
I feel your battle scars like my own
But now that they have healed
You cover yourself with a shield

We went from best friends sharing meals
To
Strangers eating on different plates

We went from inseparable
To
Separated living in different cities

We went from a perfect love story
To
Just another love crime

I am not who your family wants me to be
You are not who I need you to be

You hear my words
But you do not listen to me
When it comes to me
I take the time out of my days
To process what you hold in
And keep from me

If I mold myself into
Who you want me to be,
Would you be with me?

We met the end
I fought it
Numbing my pain
Through champagne
I kept myself together
So you would not fall apart

Even the passion of our fights
Has drained away
You repeatedly say
Everything is fine
But I cannot help but to think this is a sign
That our love has become a crime

Together we have turned into
Nothing but animated sparkles

In the hospital room
Our love is on life support
You are in bed
I am next to you
Your eyes are closed
As I stare at you

Holding your hand
Is our last touch of serenity
And I desperately pray for you to open your eyes

I so badly want to beg you to stay
But ultimately it is up to you
If you want to turn the other way

To watch you put our story on a shelf
And tuck it away like the rest

To see it collect dust
And feel its life pass from time
In fifty-five years from now
I would like to think
That if we never speak again
You will remember me as someone who
Did not fear living a life by your side

That you will remember me as someone who
Spoke with tenderness
And held your heart delicately

Past -

I open the door
To flowers on my floor
All for fondness and butterflies

Present -

I open the door
To flowers on my floor
All for forgiveness and sorrow

What used to make me full
Now turns my stomach upside down
What used to be in a vase
On my dinner table
Is now thrown straight into the trash

How his heart could stop for me
And how yours so easily
Stopped loving me

Intoxicated hearts

I was probably more drunk than sober
Our entire story
Tumbling legs
Nervous hands

It was red wine
That let us unwind

Our held-in thoughts
Became out-loud speeches
Our passion grew
Our affection became stronger

But the mornings after
Were never the same
So then came
A routine
Stiff bodies and short words
But then bottles deep we repeated
Then vulnerable hearts appeared

Take it in

He is never coming back. It is not because he doesn't love you enough; it is simply because he doesn't love himself enough.

Our love feels so long-lost
I see it in black and white
On the dance floor with no music
I thought I freed my soul
By coming to you
Only to find myself in another cage

Did you mean what you said this time?
Or was it just another accidental rage?
Are you packing your bags for life?
Or will I hear you knock on the door tomorrow?

You walk away
After making love
You shower alone now
Instead of leading me in with you by the hand
I say I love you first
Just so I can hear it back

I do not know whether to speak up
And speak my heart
I am tired of punching my steering wheel
And faking a smile

I lie to myself and say
That this is okay
All so you can stay

Is it because
The more colors showed
It was less of
Who you painted me to be?

Please tell me this is just turbulence
And not our gravesite

Shameless of my heart
As you are shameful of yours

So you blend in neatly
But the colors underneath
The ones that the world
Does not get to see
Those are rare
Those are dazzling

You pulled me away from my own heart
Replaced it with your own
You wrecked and recreated me
I will forever be yours
But you will never be just mine

I am just another art piece on the wall
In your museum
Waiting to be admired by your eyes

Impulsive love

100 miles per hour
Every firework in the world
Exploding all in my body

Half of me
Illuminated you

The whole of me
Intimidated you

Hey it's me,

I am sorry I let you down in every way I said I would not. I am sorry we had to have our last kiss and put an end to this. You were magic in the way you instantly made a home out of my heart, and even if it is abandoned now… it will always be yours. I cannot escape you. I traveled to a different country because I thought maybe distance from one another might lessen the heartache.

I was wrong, in every little thing I did and found, I thought of you. From the second I woke up in my hotel room to every street I would cross. I thought about how much the vintage cars in this town, the ambience of the underground bars, were screaming your name and how badly I wished that you were still close and not so far.

Scattered mind.

Multiple dreams and an unsettled mind
Fighting for confidence when
We do not know how to stand up straight
Overthinking young love
When it is too little too late
Lost in big cities
Relying on fate

New months feel like new days

You keep on playing the part
You tell them
We were just a friendship that faded
You murdered my heart
And covered your tracks
You were such a pure heart
Never knew you were capable of these acts

You have everything
You feel nothing
I have nothing
I feel everything

I do not love easy
We walk past thousands of hearts each day
I have touched a few lips with my own
And each time my heart caves in
I have been shown
That a good love dies fast
And the heartache feels forever-lasting

We went from
Cozy to crippling
My sanity is ripping
My tears are dripping
You threw a dart
Straight to my heart
You are healing
I am bleeding
You won
I lost

Why do I crave darkness?
Why do I crave pain?
Why do I crave you?

I often wonder how different life would be if I said more and held back less. Maybe I would have said how much your words meant to me. Instead of speaking and fighting with you, I kept it all in and fought with myself. Just maybe you would have found value in all the words I did not say.

Locking it in the vault

Part 1

Sick of me reminding you
To love me the way you say you do
The meaning of your words is disappearing
The things you do not do are damaging

Let's cry one more time to make it better
Let's cry a second so we do not become the bitter
Words we told each other
But now my tears are dry
And I despise myself
Because I am still bitter
But only because I want you to be better

I am on my rooftop
It is cold but I feel calm
We were good but we were also wrong
I dialed your number in my phone
And feel these aches in my bones
My heart is racing
I am scared of what I am facing
It destroys me to drop my pen
And not finish my idea of our love story

Part 2

It is late at night
The city has a soft glow
I see your name light up on my phone
We exchanged a few easy words
Before I spilled the heart-wrenching sentence
And then it came
The tone in your voice
Sounded like you hit a brick wall
Your mind shut down
And you kept your words small
I wanted so badly to scream, FIGHT!
But I feared that my voice
Would be mute to your ears

The phone call ended
I know we both descended
But maybe after some time
It will not only be the perfect person
But also the perfect time,
For us

Your worst will always be enough for me
But my best will never be enough for you

My new year's letter to you that I never sent.

Our hearts came from different worlds, but we proved that different worlds can blend beautifully. I thought about who my first love would be every day of my life and if I would marry them too. I will be honest: I am guilty; I always kept an eye out for who that special someone would be. You came at me from my blind side. I never would have expected someone to come out of a Palm Springs vacation, but I would not have wanted it any other way. We created some of the most magical moments of my life, and the crazy thing is that none of them were extravagant one bit. Your voice and touch were enough. I was in awe of the little things. I will never forget the night you told me you wanted me, and from word to word you said, "When I am in, I am in." And I trusted you. Some time passed, and you introduced me to your mom as your friend and I was okay with that because I knew behind closed doors I meant so much more in your heart. I constantly told you the sentence: "On your time, not mine," because I already took the time to accept myself for who I really was. I became that one person to open your eyes and make you stop ignoring your authentic roots of your soul and heart. I was honored to be that person, to show you a new life and prove that it is okay on the other side.

Listen, I get it. It is a scary thing, and it took me years to vocalize my truth. It just hurts that we had to let go of each other's hearts only because of the wrong timing, even though we knew the love was still there. It broke me to pieces the last month I was with you, watching you get eaten up inside because you did not love who you truly were inside. It kills me to the core that the last night I had with you ended with slamming doors, yelling, and screaming at each other just because I wanted you to love you… for you. That last night it was like we set our forest on fire and realized we were madly in love with each other but did not know what to do with it all. I was on one side of the fire and you were on the other, eyes connected, and you turned around and walked away as the flame caught the tip of my shirt, and I burned away.

In reality, I went to bed with tears in my eyes next to you. We woke up and acted like nothing ever happened. I packed my car to head back to Los Angeles, and you told me you would see me in a couple days, but my heart knew that was the end. Shortly after I gave you a phone call, took a deep breath, stomped on my heart to the point where I could not feel it anymore, and I told you I was done. Not because the love was gone but because I deserve a stronger love. This was the hardest day to date, but the second I hung up I felt weights lifted off my shoulder and almost like I could finally fly again. Maybe one day we will reunite when the sun is out for the both of us.

You will always have a piece of my heart. Happy new year's.

A lover can give you a key to the safe
You might feel secure
And create some of the greatest moments
Of your life

But there also might be a time
When the keys get changed
And you get locked out

Healing from a nightmare

It has been a week now, and every time I wake up, I wish it was just a nightmare. Your scent still lingers, around my home, and I have spent every minute reminiscing of the way we made each other light up.

I have taken our picture frames off my wall and held back from showing you how weak I have been. We were destined to meet and grow together, just so we can grow apart even better.

So please run away fearlessly and do not look back at me. I will sit back and watch your silhouette fade into the light.

Your lips slowly slipped off mine
And stumbled onto others

Hurt by many
You swore to god you loved me
Then one night
You had a drink too many
I closed my eyes to fall asleep
And you closed your eyes
To fall into another pair of lips

My favorite vacation

I have never traveled out of the country, but when I met you, it was like I traveled out of this world. You felt like my hometown and a vacation mixed in one. Your lips tasted like my favorite dinner and dessert. You made my heavy nights lighter; we both knew, and both of our hearts grew, for one another. It was rich in truth that together we would bring the biggest storm to exist, but we dove in head first carelessly.

At first, you were nothing but sunny days and gracious smiles. Eventually came the storms, but no matter how bad they got, we had each other. At last came the lightning that struck between us, bodies turned away in bed instead of facing each other. Paradise felt like hell, and I wanted this vacation to end. I did not know my way home, but I had to sneak away. I am now lost in the middle of nowhere and cannot tell the difference between night and day. I feel like falling, but the power of prayer is holding me up.

It is the way I wake up and look over
Wishing you were on the pillow next to me
It is the way I go on my morning coffee drives
Wishing you were in the passenger seat
And every time a good thing happens in my life
You are the first person I think to tell

I can imagine in clear color
The day my heart first fell
And now I sit back and dwell
About how I could have been better
And in what ways
I could have stopped the change

The way a love can grow
By two
And let go
By one

Marvelous but vicious

I slowed my life down for you
I held back my truth from the world
Because you were still living in a lie

The fear of showing your honest heart
To the world
Ate away our happiness
And rotted our passion
It was something that felt like forever
But it had an expiration date

We had a balance
Fancy dinners and nights in
Dancing in the kitchen
We were on different chapters
But we both took the time
To read every line
In between the pages

The more we fell
The more frightened we became
And before we knew it
We created an ocean around us
And we were in

Storm or sun we never let go
But then came a day
Where our communication and affection
Drifted away in the current

We were at dinner
The table was rumbling
The warmest heart I felt, turned cold
My head went under, and I swam deeper
My feet touched the bottom
As you reached the top
For a fresh breath of air

CONTINUED

I looked at you across the table
Your eyes were not lit up like they used to be
The rumbling table became stronger
My red glass of wine tipped over
It spilt on my clothes
And in that very moment

The wine on my shirt
Resembled all the sacrifices and hurt

Your little secret.

As the light blue sky
Slowly faded into a darker tone
As the world got quieter
You got closer

The longer I was kept a secret
The more my heart bled

It was only when the doors were locked
When no one was around
When I felt your colors light up the room

But my love was not designed
To be kept a secret

Another body in my bed feels wrong
Surface smiles and forced dates
Convinced I will never find a love as strong
How do you live so at peace
In the middle of misery?

You have always been so good at hiding it all
That I should have known
That no matter how hard I seek
I will never find the light behind your shadows

It feels like
It took a lifetime to gain the strength
To say goodbye

But I knew walking away was right
And to continue walking by your side
Would be wrong

In all the ways you could not love me
I have found it in myself
To love me

Your love was special
First time experiencing heart
That I placed before mine
You were rough on the edges
So I sculpted you smooth
Someone so soft yet so shallow
But I could not hate you
For not knowing deeper
You have never been shown how

As time went forward
You became finer
Hands and hearts latched
Everything in life seemed a bit lighter

But then came the flash of a camera
All of my favorite memories together
Became the hardest ones to see
Reality and insecurities crept in
And we no longer felt free

But I held on stronger
The world was raining glitter
We were walking on shattered glass, together
The pain hurt like hell

CONTINUED

I stood high as you fell
Instead of security
You kept me guessing
Even if you were a lesson
You were truly a blessing

Christmas under different roofs

Christmas is around the corner
We fell apart a few blocks back
Twinkling lights and presents under the tree
But it all means nothing
If you are not with me
This challenging world
Made our simple love difficult
I cannot fight against time
Nor can I press rewind
But I cannot help but to wonder
What it would have been like
To live a life with you in light
And not just when no one is in sight
To be next to you, knowing I am your man
How much stronger we would have been
If we stayed instead of ran

I imagined in my head
Waking up to you on Christmas in bed
Hot coffee and an abundance of gifts
Yet you were the most special one of them all
But in reality
Our hearts matched perfectly
At an unperfect chapter

Suddenly it all came to an end
All the memories and laughter

We are spending Christmas
Under two different roofs
I do not know where you are off to
But I wish I was there to hold you

I have fallen on the floor again
My knees feel like shattered glass
As they hit the ground

This place feels familiar
But I never thought
I would have another experience here
My heart just started fighting
As yours gave out

How dare you say
We moved too fast
When you were the driver
And I was the passenger
You said you loved me after weeks
When I waited for those three words
To stumble out of my mouth after months

Towards the end of it
I would selfishly turn around in bed
To see if you would pull me in like you used to
Back then
No more than a few hours would pass
Before you said "I miss you"
But towards the end of it
Days would pass
And I would have to say it first
Just so you could say them back

You were good to me
You cared for me
I ended my nights with your voice on the phone
And started my mornings with a text from you

The second I leave
I miss you
You say the same back
But I do not think you will ever feel
What my heart feels for you

I never knew two humans in love
Could fall apart
Simply because one loves harder
And the other could not love stronger

Learning a new love feels impossible
Everything that should feel right
Feels wrong
Everything that should feel exciting
Feels colorless
I need to give in
To what this is
Instead of living inside
Of what it was

I am in two months deep
And I have yet to take the leap
Because just maybe
You will stop running away
And you will find your way
Back into the truth of your heart

But until then
I will be here
I will not be near
But I hope you feel
That my love for you is clear

I smelled your scent on someone else yesterday
It brought back a hundred questions I never got to ask

My mind replayed the first day
You walked into my life
How are we so different from then to today?
How I saw you so pure
But then ignorance won you over

Crazy in love
Calm in hurt

You were mine again
It was decades after
From what we thought was the last chapter
Of us

But it turned out
Destiny drove us together again
We had wedding rings on our fingers
And children named after
What meant the most to us
We were a love story that once broke
Only to be made stronger

But then suddenly
The scenery started to bleed away
Your charming voice
Turned into my alarm
And my eyes opened to an empty pillow

Anyone who has been in love knows this moment:

When the romance is dead but the other half of your heart believes you can revive it. The phrase of your parents telling you when you were a kid—"You can do anything in this world"—dials into your heart. You extend your open arms and deal with the pain you are feeling only to hope a miracle will happen to a dying love. You know you need to turn and run, but you are on the floor basking the aged potion that you once both created together.

Breathe, stand strong, and walk to the graveyard of romance. Put an end date on the tombstone, lay it on the ground, and kiss it goodbye.

Hopeful to hopeless

I was too much
You were never enough

Till death do us apart
To ripping each other apart

I ran away from you
So I could run back to me

It is an odd thing watching our lives exist in two different worlds now. But maybe we were just rusted metal dipped in gold.

Letting you in
Was the better part of me
Letting you go
Was the best part of me

Biting my tongue and swallowing my blood
As you walked out
I swam and soaked in what was left
I was shattered in shadows
Only to turn around and see
That I am dazzling in sparkles

All the tears I shed
In traffic
Down the shower drain
Into my pillow
It all taught me that having emotions
Designed with delicacy
Is remarkable

You tried to climb
Your biggest mountain for me
But by the time you gave up
I was over the sky for you

We cannot live our lives thinking
About what I did
And what you did not do
I will look after you
And care for you from a distance
I hope our chapter meant something to you

I could not lie to your face
So I told you I could not live this way
I took the heart off your contact name
I bought new bed sheets
And tried a new coffee shop today

I am deeply sorry for wanting the world
To love the person
I held under the waves

I have been afraid
Of having my authentic heart
On the big screens too

I am telling you this
Because I know how scary all of it is
I told myself in the past
That if I found love
I would find myself
But I was wrong
I needed to love myself, for myself
Before I could trickle into a love story
Of two

He is everything that you are not
He does everything that you do not do
Yet I still wish it was you
When I kiss him
I feel like I am doing you wrong
When you are probably living freely
Doing whatever you want

The way
He gets excited to tell me about his day
Is the same way you used to

I prayed for someone like him
But I hate how my heart
Loves someone like you

I hope you find me there.

I miss it all
The way you would hold my hand
Driving through not only my home town
But yours too

It was all so profound
Tipsy nights leaving the bar
The way you would pull me around the corner
Your gentle touch
The intimacy held in your eyes
It all screamed "I love you"
Before you spoke those words out loud

Time is a valuable thing, if not everything
I handed over my days and nights to you
And you did too
These emotions were the first for the both of us
Our time became one

My insecurities began to write
On the walls around us
Then came your fears that painted
Over my words with white
To pretend we were alright

CONTINUED

I would hold you in for longer kisses
And tell you I loved you
A little more each day
Deep down I knew
This love could not stay

But in all the places
We added our unique color of light
I hope you find me there

I bet your lips taste better on his
Only because he is willing
To remain in your shadows

Although the shallow waters of love are safer
That is not where I intended us to be
I wanted to take risks
And get lost under the sea
So dark that we could not see

There is someone new
But I cannot stop thinking about you
I took him to all the places we used to go
And down all the pretty streets
We would drive through
But he has no clue
That I am selfish and living in déjà vu

Unevenness.

The rarity of our hearts intertwining will never be forgotten, but the thought of losing myself is more frightening than the thought of losing you. You have dimmed some of the most remarkable rooms of my soul. It is nobody's fault that mid-storm we found out there is unevenness between our love languages.

I will forever label you as a once in a lifetime kind of love. The sensation and admiration between two vulnerable souls. No words can explain how uncommon yet special you were.

Coming of age tranquility

On the days when you feel defeated
Those extra few pounds in your chest
When happiness is blurry
And sadness is in focus
Being in a constant headspace
Of wondering what went wrong
Instead of being thankful for
All the things that found their way out

Understand that you are brave. No matter how many times your heart has been mistreated and all the people who did not see your value—whether that be in love, a career opportunity, or just a silly friend that did not value your time—you are still a heart of gold. Cheers and a deep breath to the moments when you felt like taking your last breath, when you could not get out of bed to feel the sunlight, or when all the days blended into one.

You can do it, you are doing it, you will do it.
Keep running.

Self-grounding

You should never beg a lover to stay
Let them leave and if they do
It does not mean you do not have worth
It just means they cannot see it
And that is okay

Someone that is meant to be a part of your life
Will fall in the palms of your hands
All of your questions will be answered
All of your desires will be gratified
And life will finally feel simple
In the most extraordinarily way

Someone will value you

Someone will stay up a little later than usual to hear your voice after a long day.
Someone will hold you during a time of uncertainty.
Someone will listen and understand your heart.
Someone will fight for your love.

The art of self-care

Let go of the things
That make your darkness glow
And let in the ones
That feel like sunlight

You are worthy of genuine comfort and care
When you are alone
With your thoughts at 3am
Choose faith over demons

A love that ended good -

You found me in the dark
And left me in the light
Without you by my side
I never thought I would be alright

A love that felt eternal
But died young
A love that drifted into
A lesson learned

How to be brave
How to be confident

The moments when
You are biting your tongue
And one step forward
Feels like you are entering a new world

Or knowing your heart
Has been broken too many times
Yet you walk with your chin up
Ready to love stronger than before

Years after my first love and heartbreak

I have grown new flowers around me
I have created memories with special humans
And I admire that you left my life now

Be thankful for the love that creeps away
Love is meant to be promising and pure

Do not allow your past
To attach to your present

It is okay to have days
To reminisce on what was

But do not ponder on the idea
Of if

If it will happen again
If they will walk back in
If it will ever be the same again

Stunningly shattered

I had to be shattered to learn that my glass can be melted back together.

I had to be shattered to realize what really matters and how to appreciate the ground I walk on.

I had to be shattered to understand that the breaking is not the end, the sun is behind the clouds waiting for you.

If I could love you once more
I would
If I could forgive you once more
I would

But you are at fault
After so many times repairing my heart
I will not fall backwards
After multiple times when I listened to your lies
I will not brainwash myself again
After letting the true tones of love seep away
And blend into grey
I will not love a love
That is expired and rotten

When we feel the worst pain of our lives
Make sure to not cut away from it all

It is awakening your eyes
It is rebirthing your soul

I no longer will live at the bottom of the sea
Everything I lost in you
I have now found in me

I scratched you out of my idea of happiness
We were black and blue
I waited for us to heal
But over some time
It all started to reveal
That maybe it was never real

Perhaps it was two different ideas
One stagnant in the nonfiction version
While the other was in the clouds of the world of fiction
We indeed met
But maybe never fully matched
We indeed kissed
But maybe never made love

Unpredictable

Believe it or not, some of your greatest moments have yet to come. The reality is your world will stop for someone again and your heart will also ache at another point in your lifetime. But with the hurt and the chapters we close comes new and brighter love in ways we never imagined. Life is unpredictable in the most magical way.

Dating apps and endless days
Of trying to find the one that stays
Flakey dates and lovers that turn into ghosts

When did life define happiness as two?

A dinner for one
A movie night in
And a bed alone
Should always be enough
Love will follow when it is right

From a perspective of happiness

You look back and you are no longer tempted
You have been through the worst
However, your vision is turned on the good side
You have had endless nights of crying
However, from that you grew the garden of your dreams

You give people
The type of love you yearn for
A different form of pleasure

Just like a road you have never been through
And that turn you never took
A new love will enter too
The car doors held open, the surprises
It will all be made new

On the bridge
Traffic to my left
Traffic to my right
The sun is dropping
As the stars are brightening
Clarity in my mind
I found the remedy
To be healed

As we all wake up from our own beds, we have our own stories and special ways we have healed from past experiences. Some are more detrimental than others, but I oddly think that those humans stand out like art pieces in a museum, even if they do not try to.

We are all soaking in together that the simplicity of life overrules anything else. And that sometimes love between two humans in fact is not enough, and sometimes a forever gets overwritten with a temporary.

What I am trying to say is that time is precious and life is flying by. Listen to the stories that are being told around you and pause to feel your emotions regardless of the circumstance. One day we will age and speak our stories of the life we are living right now.

About the author

Ben Esqueda's writing focuses on the central themes of heartbreak, self-discovery, and coming of age. He writes to heal not only himself but the others in the world too.

You can find him on Instagram and Tiktok @benesqueda.